NABISCO

# Holiday
# Appetizers & More

pil

Publications International, Ltd.

Favorite Brand Name Recipes at www.fbnr.com

**Kraft Kitchens Manager:** Marianne Arimenta-Dente

Pictured on the front cover: Roasted Red Pepper-Basil Spread *(page 12)*.
Pictured on the back cover: Pinecone Cheese Spread *(page 36)*.

ISBN-13: 978-1-4127-7718-6
ISBN-10: 1-4127-7718-6

Manufactured in China.

8 7 6 5 4 3 2 1

**Nutritional Analysis:** Every effort has been made to check the accuracy of the nutritional information that appears with each recipe. However, because numerous variables account for a wide range of values for certain foods, nutritive analyses in this book should be considered approximate. Different results may be obtained by using different nutrient databases and different brand-name products.

**Microwave Cooking:** Microwave ovens vary in wattage. Use the cooking times as guidelines and check for doneness before adding more time.

**Preparation/Cooking Times:** Preparation times are based on the approximate amount of time required to assemble the recipe before cooking, baking, chilling or serving. These times include preparation steps such as measuring, chopping and mixing. The fact that some preparations and cooking can be done simultaneously is taken into account. Preparation of optional ingredients and serving suggestions is not included.

# Contents

16

56

72

*D*uring the holiday season, parties and family gatherings are all about spending time with the people you love. Whatever holiday you celebrate, food plays an important role in many gatherings.

Most people love to reconnect with family and friends, and planning and preparing the special treats for holiday gatherings provides the opportunity to nurture these special connections. With this in mind, the special food ideas in this booklet can be quickly and easily prepared using familiar ingredients, along with your favorite **NABISCO** Crackers. In *Celebration Starters, Mix 'n Mingle Dips & Spreads, and Crowd-Pleasing Cracker Toppings*, you'll find a wide range of easy-to-prepare hearty appetizers, snacks, dips, and spreads. Not only will they satisfy your guests, but they'll also ensure that you won't miss the party yourself! We start with the great flavor and crunch of **TRISCUIT** Crackers, made with 100% whole grains and zero trans fat, **RITZ** Crackers, with their buttery, melt-in-your-mouth flavor and flaky crunch, and the multi-dimensional flavor of **WHEAT THINS** Snack Crackers. Their shapes, flavors, and textures complement the creamy and savory selection of dips, spreads, and toppings perfectly. Furthermore, if looking for better-for-you options, check the nutrition information to find recipes that meet your goals.

We have included some show-stopping desserts in *Tasteful Traditions*, along with simple tips for presenting your food with style and pizzazz. With the goodness of **NILLA** Wafers, **OREO** Chocolate Sandwich Cookies and **HONEY MAID** Honey Grahams, these wonderful family pleasers are deliciously simple. They're perfect for parties since they can be assembled ahead of time and decorated just before serving. Lastly, *Gift-Giving Favorites* is dedicated to the creation of homemade gifts from your very own kitchen. We hope that you enjoy preparing these as much as we enjoyed creating them for you and your family.

As you plan ahead for the holiday season, these recipes can help you entertain with a savvy, sophisticated style while you create lasting memories and have fun at your own parties!

**Marianne Arimenta-Dente**
*Kraft Kitchens*

Triscuit®

Nilla wafers

OREO

RITZ

Honey Maid GRAHAMS

Wheat Thins®

# CELEBRATION

### Extra-special appetizers for those extra-special holiday gatherings

# STARTERS

## SHRIMP SPREAD

Prep: 15 min. ● Total: 15 min.

1 lb. frozen peeled and deveined shrimp (41 to 50 count), cooked, divided

1 pkg. (8 oz.) **PHILADELPHIA** Cream Cheese, softened

¾ cup finely chopped celery

¼ cup finely chopped stuffed green olives

**RITZ** Crackers

**CHOP** enough shrimp to measure 1 cup; place in medium bowl. Set remaining shrimp aside for later use.

**ADD** cream cheese, celery and olives to shrimp in bowl; mix well. Spoon onto center of serving plate. Shape into 6-inch round. Arrange remaining shrimp around edge of cream cheese mixture, pressing gently into cream cheese mixture to secure.

**SERVE** with crackers.

*Makes 16 servings, 2 Tbsp. spread and 5 crackers each.*

**Nutrition Information Per Serving:** 160 calories, 10g total fat, 4g saturated fat, 310mg sodium, 11 g carbohydrate, 8g protein.

## How to Devein Raw Shrimp:

To devein raw shrimp, remove the outer shell first. Then make a lengthwise shallow cut on the outer curve of the shrimp. (This will expose the black vein.) Loosen the vein with the tip of a sharp knife and then pull with your fingers to completely remove.

# SOUTHERN-STYLE CRAB CAKES WITH COOL LIME SAUCE

Prep: 15 min. ● Total: 23 min.

Grated peel and juice from 1 lime, divided

1 cup **KRAFT** Mayo Real Mayonnaise or **MIRACLE WHIP** Dressing, divided

1 env. **GOOD SEASONS** Italian Salad Dressing & Recipe Mix

2 Tbsp. **GREY POUPON** Country Dijon Mustard

2 cans (6 oz. each) crabmeat, drained, flaked

25 **RITZ** Crackers, finely crushed, divided

1 green onion, chopped

¼ cup **BREAKSTONE'S** or **KNUDSEN** Sour Cream

**MIX** half of the lime juice, ½ cup of the mayo, the salad dressing mix and mustard in medium bowl until well blended. Add crabmeat, ½ cup of the cracker crumbs and the onion; mix lightly.

**SHAPE** into 18 (½-inch-thick) patties; coat with remaining cracker crumbs.

**COOK** patties in batches in large nonstick skillet on medium heat 2 min. on each side or until browned on both sides and heated through. Meanwhile, mix remaining ½ cup mayo, remaining lime juice, the lime peel and sour cream until well blended. Serve with crab cakes.

*Makes 18 servings, 1 crab cake and 2 tsp. sauce each.*

Note: If skillet is not nonstick, cook crab cakes in 1 Tbsp. oil.

**Nutrition Information Per Serving:** 140 calories, 12g total fat, 2g saturated fat, 340mg sodium, 4g carbohydrate, 4g protein.

# Jazz It Up:

Spoon sauce decoratively onto serving plate before topping with crab cake. Garnish with a lime slice and additional chopped green onions.

# ROASTED RED PEPPER-BASIL SPREAD

Prep: 15 min. ● Total: 1 hour 15 min. (incl. refrigerating)

- 1 tub (12 oz.) **PHILADELPHIA** Cream Cheese Spread
- ¼ cup lightly packed fresh basil leaves
- 1 clove garlic, peeled
- ¼ cup drained roasted red peppers
- 5 pitted black olives, chopped
- 2 Tbsp. **PLANTERS** Sliced Almonds, toasted
- **RITZ** Crackers

**PLACE** cream cheese spread in blender; set aside. Wash tub; line with plastic wrap, with ends of wrap extending over side of tub. Set aside.

**ADD** basil and garlic to cream cheese in blender; cover. Blend using pulsing action until well blended; set aside. Cut a star shape from one of the peppers, using ½-inch star-shaped cutter; set star aside for later use. Chop pepper trimmings and remaining peppers; combine with the olives. Spoon ½ cup of the cream cheese mixture into prepared tub. Cover with the chopped pepper mixture; press lightly into cream cheese mixture. Top with the remaining cream cheese mixture; cover. Refrigerate 1 hour.

**UNMOLD** cheese spread onto serving plate; remove and discard plastic wrap. Top cheese spread with the almonds and pepper star. Serve as a spread with the crackers.

*Makes 1½ cups or 12 servings, 2 Tbsp. spread and 5 crackers each.*

**Make Ahead:** Prepare cheese spread as directed. Cover and refrigerate up to 24 hours. Unmold and continue as directed.

**Nutrition Information Per Serving:** 180 calories, 13g total fat, 6g saturated fat, 300mg sodium, 12g carbohydrate, 3g protein.

## Jazz It Up:

For a holiday flair, serve with RITZ SIMPLY SOCIALS Crackers.

# EASY RITZ HOT WINGS

Prep: 20 min. ● Total: 1 hour

**1** sleeve **RITZ** Crackers (38 crackers), finely crushed

**1** tsp. dried oregano leaves

**½** tsp. garlic powder

**½** tsp. paprika

**⅛** tsp. coarsely ground black pepper

**2** lb. chicken wings, separated at joints, tips discarded

**½** cup hot pepper sauce

**PREHEAT** oven to 350°F. Mix cracker crumbs and seasonings in shallow dish.

**COAT** chicken with hot pepper sauce, then dip in crumb mixture, turning to evenly coat both sides of each wing piece. Place in single layer on greased baking sheet.

**BAKE** 35 to 40 min. or until golden brown and cooked through (165°F), turning pieces over after 20 min. Serve warm.

*Makes 20 servings, about 1 chicken wing each.*

**Nutrition Information Per Serving:** 120 calories, 7g total fat, 2g saturated fat, 160mg sodium, 4g carbohydrate, 8g protein.

## Serving Suggestion:

Serve these flavorful appetizers with vegetable sticks and KRAFT ROKA Blue Cheese Dressing.

# CRANBERRY AND PECAN CHEESE LOG

Prep: 15 min. ● Total: 45 min. (incl. refrigerating)

**1** container (8 oz.) **PHILADELPHIA** Light Cream Cheese Spread

**¼** cup chopped dried cranberries

**1** Tbsp. grated orange peel

**½** cup coarsely chopped **PLANTERS** Pecans, toasted

**TRISCUIT** Rosemary & Olive Oil Crackers

**MIX** cream cheese spread, cranberries and orange peel until well blended. Shape into 6-inch log.

**ROLL** in pecans until evenly coated on all sides. Wrap tightly in plastic wrap.

**REFRIGERATE** at least 30 min. Serve as a spread with the crackers.

*Makes 1½ cups or 12 servings, 2 Tbsp. spread and 6 crackers each.*

**Nutrition Information Per Serving:** 200 calories, 10g total fat, 2.5g saturated fat, 220mg sodium, 24g carbohydrate, 5g protein.

*Take Along:*

Bringing this colorful cheese log to a holiday party? Remember to pack a copy of the recipe. You're sure to get requests!

# SHALLOT & BACON BRIE

Prep: 10 min. ● Total: 11 min.

**2** slices **OSCAR MAYER** Bacon

**2** shallots, thinly sliced

**2** tsp. **GREY POUPON** Savory Honey Mustard

**1** wheel Brie cheese (8 oz.)

**RITZ** Crackers

**COOK** bacon in nonstick skillet on medium heat until crisp. Drain bacon, reserving drippings in skillet; set bacon aside.

**ADD** shallots to bacon drippings in skillet; cook until shallots are tender, stirring frequently. Crumble bacon into small bowl. Add shallot mixture and mustard; mix well. Spoon over cheese in microwaveable serving dish.

**MICROWAVE** on HIGH 45 sec. or just until cheese is warmed. Serve as a spread with the crackers.

*Makes 16 servings, 2 Tbsp. spread and 5 crackers each.*

**Nutrition Information Per Serving:** 150 calories, 10g total fat, 4g saturated fat, 270mg sodium, 12g carbohydrate, 5g protein.

## The Perfect Cheese Tray:

Cheese trays are ideal for entertaining. Be sure to include a selection of KRAFT Cheeses in mild, medium and strong flavors. Cut cheeses into an assortment of shapes, then arrange on a large tray or platter along with a sampling of NABISCO crackers and colorful fresh fruit.

# THE ULTIMATE STUFFED MUSHROOM

Prep: 20 min. ● Total: 35 min.

20 mushrooms

3 Tbsp. butter

2 Tbsp. finely chopped onions

2 Tbsp. finely chopped red peppers

14 **RITZ** Crackers, finely crushed (about ½ cup crumbs)

2 Tbsp. **KRAFT** 100% Grated Parmesan Cheese

½ tsp. Italian seasoning

**PREHEAT** oven to 400°F. Remove stems from mushrooms. Finely chop enough of the stems to measure ¼ cup; set aside. Cover and refrigerate remaining stems for other use.

**MELT** butter in large skillet on medium heat. Add ¼ cup chopped mushroom stems, the onions and peppers; cook and stir until vegetables are tender. Stir in cracker crumbs, cheese and Italian seasoning. Spoon crumb mixture evenly into mushroom caps. Place on baking sheet.

**BAKE** 15 min. or until heated through.

*Makes 20 servings, 1 stuffed mushroom each.*

**Make Ahead:** Mushrooms can be stuffed several hours in advance. Cover and refrigerate until ready to serve. Uncover and bake at 400°F for 20 min. or until heated through.

**Nutrition Information Per Serving:** 35 calories, 2.5g total fat, 1g saturated fat, 45mg sodium, 2g carbohydrate, 1g protein.

## Make It Easy:

When preparing mushrooms for stuffing, use a melon baller to carefully scoop a little mushroom flesh from the cap after removing the stem. Then use the melon baller to easily scoop the filling mixture into the mushrooms.

# ROASTED EGGPLANT CAPONATA

Prep: 1 hour 10 min. ● Total: 3 hours 10 min. (incl. refrigerating)

**1 head garlic**

**1 Tbsp. olive oil**

**1 large eggplant (1½ lb.)**

**1 can (14½ oz.) diced tomatoes, drained**

**¼ cup chopped fresh parsley**

**2 Tbsp. chopped red onions**

**2 Tbsp. balsamic vinegar**

**¼ tsp. salt**

**1 Tbsp. KRAFT Shredded Parmesan Cheese**

**WHEAT THINS Snack Crackers**

**PREHEAT** oven to 375°F. Cut ½-inch-thick slice off top of garlic, exposing cloves; discard top. Brush cut-side of garlic lightly with oil; wrap tightly in foil. Place on ungreased baking sheet. Pierce eggplant in several places with fork or sharp knife. Place on baking sheet with garlic. Bake 50 min. to 1 hour or until both are tender; cool slightly.

**PEEL** eggplant; cut into small pieces. Place in medium bowl. Mince 3 of the garlic cloves. Add to eggplant along with the tomatoes, parsley, onions, vinegar and salt; mix well. Cover; refrigerate at least 2 hours. Meanwhile, store remaining garlic in refrigerator for another use.

**SPRINKLE** eggplant mixture with cheese just before serving. Serve as a dip with the crackers.

*Makes 2 cups or 16 servings, 2 Tbsp. dip and 16 crackers each.*

**How to Serve Warm:** Just before serving, spoon the dip into microwaveable bowl. Microwave on HIGH 1 min., stirring after 30 sec.

**Nutrition Information Per Serving:** 170 calories, 7g total fat, 1g saturated fat, 320mg sodium, 24g carbohydrate, 3g protein.

*Creative Leftovers:*

Store leftover roasted garlic in tightly covered container in refrigerator. Spread onto your favorite NABISCO Crackers, then top with any leftover eggplant mixture.

# MARINATED FETA CHEESE

Prep: 10 min. ● Total: 1 hour 10 min. (incl. refrigerating)

1 pkg. (8 oz.) **ATHENOS** Traditional Feta Cheese

2 Tbsp. **GOOD SEASONS** Italian Vinaigrette with Extra Virgin Olive Oil Dressing

1 tsp. finely chopped fennel tops

1 tsp. finely chopped fresh rosemary

¼ tsp. crushed red pepper

¼ tsp. grated lemon peel

**CUT** cheese into 32 cubes; place in medium bowl.

**ADD** remaining ingredients; mix lightly. Cover.

**REFRIGERATE** at least 1 hour.

*Makes 8 servings, 4 cheese cubes each.*

**Make Ahead:** Cheese mixture can be refrigerated up to 24 hours before serving.

**Nutrition Information Per Serving (cheese only):** 80 calories, 7g total fat, 4.5g saturated fat, 360mg sodium, 1g carbohydrate, 5g protein.

## Serving Suggestion:

Serve with **SOCIABLES** Savory Crackers, **RITZ** Snowflake Crackers or **RITZ SIMPLY SOCIALS** Crackers.

# MIX 'N MINGLE DIPS &

**Make these recipes ahead of time and enjoy the party with your guests!**

# SPREADS

## LAYERED PESTO AND RED PEPPER DIP

Prep: 15 min. ● Total: 1 hour 15 min. (incl. refrigerating)

1 tub (8 oz.) **PHILADELPHIA** Light Cream Cheese Spread, divided

¼ cup chopped drained roasted red peppers

1 Tbsp. pesto

1 Tbsp. milk

**WHEAT THINS** Snack Crackers

**PLACE** half of the cream cheese spread and the peppers in blender; cover. Blend 30 to 40 sec. or until well blended, stopping and scraping down side of blender as needed.

**MIX** remaining cream cheese spread, pesto and milk until well blended. Spread onto small serving plate; top with the red pepper mixture. Cover.

**REFRIGERATE** at least 1 hour before serving.

*Makes about 1 cup or 9 servings, 2 Tbsp. dip and 16 crackers each.*

Make Ahead: The 2 layers of dip can be made up to 1 day ahead and stored in separate tightly covered containers in the refrigerator. For best results, layer the dips no more than 2 hours before serving.

**Nutrition Information Per Serving:** 210 calories, 10g total fat, 3g saturated fat, 420mg sodium, 23g carbohydrate, 5g protein.

# HOT APPLE PIE DIP

Prep: 10 min. ● Total: 22 min.

- **1** tub (8 oz.) **PHILADELPHIA** Light Cream Cheese Spread
- **2** Tbsp. brown sugar
- **½** tsp. pumpkin pie spice
- **1** apple, chopped, divided
- **¼** cup **KRAFT** 2% Milk Shredded Reduced Fat Cheddar Cheese
- **1** Tbsp. finely chopped **PLANTERS** Pecan Pieces

  **WHEAT THINS** Lightly Cinnamon Snack Crackers

**PREHEAT** oven to 375°F. Mix cream cheese spread, sugar and spice in medium bowl until well blended. Stir in half of the chopped apple.

**SPREAD** into 8-inch pie plate or small casserole dish. Top with remaining apples, the Cheddar cheese and pecans.

**BAKE** 10 to 12 min. or until heated through. Serve with the crackers.

*Makes 2 cups or 16 servings, 2 Tbsp. dip and 15 crackers each.*

**Substitute:** Substitute ground cinnamon for the pumpkin pie spice.

**Nutrition Information Per Serving:** 190 calories, 8g total fat, 2.5g saturated fat, 210mg sodium, 25g carbohydrate, 4g protein.

# LAYERED HOT ARTICHOKE AND FETA DIP

Prep: 10 min. ● Total: 30 min.

1  pkg. (8 oz.) **PHILADELPHIA** Neufchâtel Cheese, ⅓ Less Fat than Cream Cheese, softened

1  can (14 oz.) artichoke hearts, drained, chopped

½  cup **KRAFT** Shredded Parmesan Cheese

2  cloves garlic, minced

1  small red pepper, chopped

1  pkg. (3.5 oz.) **ATHENOS** Crumbled Reduced Fat Feta Cheese

1  Tbsp. sliced black olives

 **WHEAT THINS** Toasted Chips Multi-Grain

**PREHEAT** oven to 350°F. Mix Neufchâtel cheese, artichokes, Parmesan cheese and garlic until well blended.

**SPREAD** into 3-cup ovenproof serving dish; top with peppers and feta cheese.

**BAKE** 20 min.; top with olives. Serve with the chips.

*Makes 3 cups or 24 servings, 2 Tbsp. dip and 15 chips each.*

**Make Ahead:** Assemble dip as directed; cover and refrigerate up to 8 hours. When ready to serve, uncover and bake at 350°F for 25 min. or until heated through.

**Nutrition Information Per Serving:** 170 calories, 7g total fat, 2.5g saturated fat, 500mg sodium, 22g carbohydrate, 5g protein.

# CHUNKY VEGETABLE HUMMUS

Prep: 10 min. ● Total: 10 min.

  1  container (7 oz.) **ATHENOS** Original Hummus

  ¾  cup chopped, peeled and seeded cucumbers

  ¼  cup chopped red onions

  1  plum tomato, chopped

  ¼  cup **ATHENOS** Traditional Crumbled Feta Cheese

     **WHEAT THINS** Big Snack Crackers

**SPREAD** hummus onto serving plate.

**TOP** with layers of cucumbers, onions and tomatoes; sprinkle with cheese.

**SERVE** with the crackers.

*Makes 2½ cups or 20 servings, 2 Tbsp. dip and 11 crackers each.*

Substitute: Prepare as directed, using **ATHENOS** Crumbled Reduced Fat Feta Cheese.

**Nutrition Information Per Serving:** 170 calories, 7g total fat, 1.5g saturated fat, 350mg sodium, 24g carbohydrate, 3g protein.

*Shortcut:*

Save time by preparing with already-chopped vegetables purchased at the salad bar in your local supermarket.

# CHEESY SPINACH AND ARTICHOKE DIP

Prep: 10 min. ● Total: 30 min.

1  can (14 oz.) artichoke hearts, drained, finely chopped

1  pkg. (10 oz.) frozen chopped spinach, thawed, drained

¾  cup **KRAFT** 100% Grated Parmesan Cheese

¾  cup **KRAFT** Mayo Light Mayonnaise

½  cup **KRAFT** 2% Milk Shredded Reduced Fat Mozzarella Cheese

½  tsp. garlic powder

   **WHEAT THINS** Toasted Chips Multi-Grain

**PREHEAT** oven to 350°F. Mix all ingredients except chips until well blended.

**SPOON** into 9-inch pie plate or quiche dish.

**BAKE** 20 min. or until heated through. Serve with the chips.

*Makes 2¾ cups or 22 servings, 2 Tbsp. dip and 15 chips each.*

**Nutrition Information Per Serving:** 190 calories, 9g total fat, 2g saturated fat, 500mg sodium, 23g carbohydrate, 5g protein.

## Variation:

Awesome Spinach and Mushroom Dip: Substitute 1 cup chopped mushrooms for the artichoke hearts.

# PINECONE CHEESE SPREAD

Prep: 20 min. • Total: 2 hours 35 min. (incl. refrigerating)

1 pkg. (8 oz.) **PHILADELPHIA** Cream Cheese, softened

1 pkg. (8 oz.) **KRAFT** 2% Milk Shredded Reduced Fat Four Cheese Mexican Style Cheese

2 Tbsp. **GREY POUPON** Dijon Mustard

2 Tbsp. chopped canned green chilies

⅓ cup **PLANTERS** Sliced Almonds, toasted

**RITZ** Crackers

**PLACE** cream cheese, shredded cheese and mustard in food processor or blender; cover. Process until well blended. Stir in chilies.

**PLACE** on sheet of waxed paper; shape into 4-inch oval to resemble a pinecone. Insert almonds in rows to completely cover cream cheese mixture; cover.

**REFRIGERATE** 2 hours or until firm. Let stand at room temperature 15 min. before serving with the crackers.

*Makes 2 cups or 16 servings, 2 Tbsp. spread and 5 crackers each.*

**Make Ahead:** Spread can be stored, tightly covered, in refrigerator up to 5 days.

**Substitute:** Serve with **RITZ** Snowflake Crackers.

**Nutrition Information Per Serving:** 190 calories, 13g total fat, 6g saturated fat, 360mg sodium, 11 g carbohydrate, 6g protein.

## Jazz It Up:

Prepare as directed, adding 1 tsp. hot pepper sauce to the cream cheese mixture before shaping as directed.

# HOT HOLIDAY BROCCOLI DIP

Prep: 10 min. • Total: 40 min.

**1 cup MIRACLE WHIP Light Dressing**

**1 pkg. (10 oz.) frozen chopped broccoli, thawed, well drained**

**1 jar (2 oz.) diced pimientos, drained**

**½ cup KRAFT 100% Grated Parmesan Cheese**

**1 cup KRAFT 2% Milk Shredded Reduced Fat Mozzarella Cheese, divided**

**WHEAT THINS Snack Crackers**

**PREHEAT** oven to 350°F. Combine dressing, broccoli, pimientos, Parmesan cheese and ½ cup of the mozzarella cheese.

**SPREAD** into baking dish or 9-inch pie plate.

**BAKE** 20 to 25 min. or until heated through. Sprinkle with remaining ½ cup mozzarella cheese. Bake an additional 5 min. or until mozzarella cheese is melted. Serve with the crackers.

*Makes about 3 cups or 25 servings, about 2 Tbsp. dip and 16 crackers each.*

**Nutrition Information Per Serving:** 180 calories, 8g total fat, 2g saturated fat, 440mg sodium, 23g carbohydrate, 5g protein.

## Time-Out:

Take a time-out during the busy holiday season to watch a movie or two! Pick a holiday classic or something that's guaranteed to make you laugh. Prepare your favorite snack and enjoy!

# CHEESY HOT CRAB AND RED PEPPER DIP

Prep: 10 min. ● Total: 30 min.

1½  cups **KRAFT** 2% Milk Shredded Reduced Fat Mozzarella Cheese, divided

1 pkg. (8 oz.) **PHILADELPHIA** Neufchâtel Cheese, ⅓ Less Fat than Cream Cheese, softened

1 tsp. garlic powder

1 tsp. Italian seasoning

1 medium red pepper, chopped

1 small onion, finely chopped

1 can (6 oz.) crabmeat, drained

**WHEAT THINS** Snack Crackers

**PREHEAT** oven to 375°F. Remove ½ cup of the mozzarella cheese; cover and refrigerate until ready to use. Mix all remaining ingredients except crackers until well blended.

**SPREAD** into 9-inch pie plate.

**BAKE** 20 min. or until crab mixture is heated through and top is lightly browned. Sprinkle with reserved ½ cup mozzarella cheese. Serve hot with the crackers.

*Makes 3 cups or 24 servings, 2 Tbsp. dip and 16 crackers each.*

**Substitute:** Prepare as directed, using **PHILADELPHIA** Cream Cheese and **KRAFT** Shredded Mozzarella Cheese. Serve with **WHEAT THINS** Toasted Chips Multi-Grain or **RITZ** Toasted Chips.

**Nutrition Information Per Serving:** 200 calories, 9g total fat, 3g saturated fat, 380mg sodium, 22g carbohydrate, 7g protein.

# APPLE, PECAN & BLUE CHEESE SPREAD

Prep: 10 min. ● Total: 2 hours 10 min. (incl. refrigerating)

**1** container (8 oz.) **PHILADELPHIA** Light Cream Cheese Spread

**½** cup **BREAKSTONE'S** Reduced Fat or **KNUDSEN** Light Sour Cream

**1** Rome Beauty apple, finely chopped

**¼** cup **ATHENOS** Crumbled Blue Cheese

**¼** cup chopped red onion

**¼** cup chopped toasted **PLANTERS** Pecans

**TRISCUIT** Crackers

**BEAT** cream cheese spread and sour cream in medium bowl until well blended.

**ADD** apples, blue cheese, onions and pecans; mix well. Cover.

**REFRIGERATE** at least 2 hours. Serve as a spread with the crackers.

*Makes 3 cups or 24 servings, 2 Tbsp. spread and 6 crackers each.*

**Nutrition Information Per Serving:** 170 calories, 8g total fat, 2.5g saturated fat, 250mg sodium, 22g carbohydrate, 4g protein.

## Serving Suggestion:

For a unique dip container, cut top off and hollow out a large red apple. Stand upright on serving platter and fill with dip just before serving. Surround with crackers.

# CHEESY CHRISTMAS TREE

Prep: 10 min. ● Total: 10 min.

**1 pkg. (8 oz.) PHILADELPHIA Cream Cheese**

**½ cup pesto**

**¼ cup chopped red peppers**

**1 stick KRAFT POLLY-O TWIST-UMS String Cheese**

**RITZ Crackers**

**CUT** block of cream cheese diagonally in half. Arrange both halves, with points together, on serving plate to resemble Christmas-tree shape.

**CUT** a 2-inch piece from the string cheese. Place at bottom of tree for the trunk. Wrap up remaining string cheese; refrigerate until ready to use for snacking or other use.

**SPOON** pesto over cream cheese; sprinkle with peppers. Serve as a spread with the crackers.

*Makes 1½ cups or 12 servings, 2 Tbsp. spread and 5 crackers each.*

**Substitute:** Prepare as directed, using **PHILADELPHIA** Neufchâtel Cheese, ⅓ Less Fat than Cream Cheese.

**Nutrition Information Per Serving:** 200 calories, 16g total fat, 6g saturated fat, 280mg sodium, 12g carbohydrate, 3g protein.

# CROWD-PLEASING CRACKER

**Perfect pairings of crunchy crackers
and special toppings for
your most elegant gatherings**

# TOPPINGS

## "BRUSCHETTA" TRISCUIT

Prep: 10 min. ● Total: 10 min.

- **1 small tomato, finely chopped (about ½ cup)**
- **¼ cup KRAFT 2% Milk Shredded Reduced Fat Mozzarella Cheese**
- **3 Tbsp. sliced green onions**
- **1 Tbsp. KRAFT Light Zesty Italian Reduced Fat Dressing**
- **40 TRISCUIT Crackers**
- **1 pkg. (8 oz.) PHILADELPHIA Neufchâtel Cheese, ⅓ Less Fat than Cream Cheese, softened**

**MIX** tomatoes, cheese, onions and dressing.

**SPREAD** each cracker with about 1 tsp. of the Neufchâtel cheese; top with 1 tsp. of the tomato mixture.

*Makes 20 servings, 2 topped crackers each.*

**Make Ahead:** Prepare tomato mixture as directed. Add Neufchâtel cheese; mix well. Cover and refrigerate up to 24 hours. Spread onto crackers just before serving.

**Nutrition Information Per Serving:** 70 calories, 4.5g total fat, 2g saturated fat, 130mg sodium, 7g carbohydrate, 2g protein.

# CAPRESE TOPPER

Prep: 5 min. ● Total: 12 min.

 **4** oz. **POLLY**-O Part Skim Mozzarella Cheese, cut into **9** slices

**18** **TRISCUIT** Fire Roasted Tomato & Olive Oil Crackers

 **2** plum tomatoes, cut into **9** slices each

 **1** Tbsp. pesto

**18** small fresh basil leaves

**PREHEAT** oven to 350°F. Cut each cheese slice in half.

**TOP** crackers with cheese and tomatoes. Place on baking sheet.

**BAKE** 5 to 7 min. or until cheese is melted. Top with pesto and basil. Serve warm.

*Makes 1½ doz. or 9 servings, 2 topped crackers each.*

**Serving Suggestion:** When serving appetizers, offer a variety of colors, shapes and flavors. Include an assortment of dips, cracker toppers and spreads in both hot and cold forms.

**Nutrition Information Per Serving:** 90 calories, 4.5g total fat, 2g saturated fat, 160mg sodium, 8g carbohydrate, 5g protein.

# SHRIMP APPETIZERS WITH GREEN MAYONNAISE

Prep: 20 min. ● Total: 1 hour 20 min. (incl. refrigerating)

¼ cup **KRAFT** Mayo Light Mayonnaise

2 Tbsp. minced fresh parsley

1 Tbsp. finely chopped green onion

½ tsp. grated lime peel

18 shrimp (31 to 40 count), cleaned, cooked

18 **WHEAT THINS** Big Snack Crackers

**MIX** mayo, parsley, onion and lime peel in medium bowl. Add shrimp; toss to evenly coat. Cover.

**REFRIGERATE** at least 1 hour.

**SPOON** onto crackers just before serving.

*Makes 1½ doz. or 6 servings, 3 topped crackers each.*

**Substitute:** Prepare as directed, using **RITZ** Crackers or **TRISCUIT** Crackers.

**Shrimp Sizes:** The size of a shrimp is indicated by the number of shrimp per pound. The smaller the number, the larger the shrimp. Less than 15 is jumbo shrimp; 16 to 20 is extra-large shrimp; 21 to 30 is large shrimp; and 31 to 40 is medium shrimp.

**Nutrition Information Per Serving (without garnish):** 90 calories, 5g total fat, 1g saturated fat, 190mg sodium, 7g carbohydrate, 3g protein.

## Jazz It Up:

Top each appetizer with small strips of roasted red peppers and a parsley sprig.

# ARTICHOKE-CHEESE PUFFS

Prep: 10 min. ● Total: 50 min. (incl. refrigerating)

36 **RITZ** Crackers, divided

1 pkg. (8 oz.) **PHILADELPHIA** Cream Cheese, softened

¼ cup **KRAFT** 100% Grated Parmesan Cheese

¼ cup **KRAFT** 2% Milk Shredded Reduced Fat Mozzarella Cheese

½ cup chopped drained canned artichoke hearts

**CRUSH** 4 of the crackers. Place in shallow dish; set aside. Mix cheeses and artichokes until well blended. Shape 2 tsp. of the cheese mixture into ball. (If cheese mixture is too soft, cover and refrigerate until firm enough to shape into ball.) Repeat with remaining cheese mixture to make a total of 32 balls. Roll in cracker crumbs until evenly coated. Place in single layer on wax paper-covered tray; cover. Refrigerate 30 min.

**PREHEAT** oven to 350°F. Arrange remaining 32 crackers in single layer on baking sheet; top each with 1 cheese ball.

**BAKE** 10 min. or until heated through.

*Makes 16 servings, 2 cheese puffs each.*

**Shortcut:** Serve these delicious appetizers cold. Prepare cheese balls as directed and refrigerate up to 24 hours. Place 1 cheese ball on each cracker just before serving.

**Substitute:** Prepare as directed, using **RITZ** Snowflake Crackers.

**Nutrition Information Per Serving (with cracker crumb coating):** 100 calories, 8g total fat, 4g saturated fat, 200mg sodium, 6g carbohydrate, 3g protein.

## Jazz It Up:

Try adding one of the following to the cracker crumbs: toasted sesame seeds; chopped fresh dill or fresh chives; finely chopped red, green and yellow peppers. Or omit the crumbs and coat only in the alternative coating.

# RED ONION-BALSAMIC TOPPER

Prep: 10 min. ● Total: 52 min.

**1** **Tbsp. olive oil**

**1** **red onion, thinly sliced (about 1 cup)**

**2** **Tbsp. balsamic vinegar**

**48** **TRISCUIT Rosemary & Olive Oil Crackers**

**¼** **cup BREAKSTONE'S Reduced Fat or KNUDSEN Light Sour Cream**

**HEAT** oil in large skillet on medium heat. Add onions; cook 10 min. or until tender, stirring frequently. Stir in vinegar; cook an additional 1 to 2 min. or until vinegar is evaporated. Cool.

**SPOON** 1 tsp. of the onion mixture onto each cracker; top with ¼ tsp. of the sour cream.

**SERVE** warm.

*Makes 4 doz. or 16 servings, 3 topped crackers each.*

**Creative Leftovers:** For a heartier appetizer, top each cracker with a thin slice of leftover cooked steak before covering with the onion mixture and sour cream.

**Nutrition Information Per Serving:** 80 calories, 3.5g total fat, 0.5g saturated fat, 70mg sodium, 11g carbohydrate, 2g protein.

## Jazz It Up:

**Garnish topped crackers with chopped fresh parsley.**

# TUSCAN CHICKEN BITES

Prep: 15 min. ● Total: 1 hour 15 min. (incl. refrigerating)

**1** small boneless, skinless chicken breast half (4 oz.), cooked, finely chopped (about ¾ cup)

**¼** cup **BREAKSTONE'S FREE** or **KNUDSEN FREE** Fat Free Sour Cream

**2** green onions, finely chopped

**2** Tbsp. finely chopped roasted red peppers

**1** tsp. grated lemon peel

**½** tsp. chopped fresh rosemary

**24** **TRISCUIT** Cracked Pepper & Olive Oil Crackers

**24** baby arugula leaves

**COMBINE** all ingredients except crackers and arugula; cover.

**REFRIGERATE** at least 1 hour.

**TOP** each cracker with 1 arugula leaf and 2 tsp. of the chicken mixture just before serving.

*Makes 2 doz. or 8 servings, 3 topped crackers each.*

**Substitute:** Prepare as directed, substituting 2 small marinated sun-dried tomatoes, finely chopped, for the roasted red peppers.

**Nutrition Information Per Serving:** 90 calories, 2.5g total fat, 0g saturated fat, 105mg sodium, 12g carbohydrate, 5g protein.

# RITZ CHEESY-CRAB TOPPER

Prep: 10 min. ● Total: 1 hour 10 min. (incl. refrigerating)

 4  oz. (½ of 8 oz. pkg.) **PHILADELPHIA** Cream Cheese, softened

 ¼  cup **BREAKSTONE'S** or **KNUDSEN** Sour Cream

 1  can (6 oz.) crabmeat, drained, flaked

 ¼  cup chopped fresh parsley

 1  Tbsp. **KRAFT** 100% Grated Parmesan Cheese

 3  drops hot pepper sauce

48  **RITZ** Crackers

**MIX** all ingredients except crackers; cover.

**REFRIGERATE** at least 1 hour.

**SPOON** about 1 tsp. of the crabmeat mixture onto each cracker just before serving.

*Makes 4 doz. or 16 servings, 3 topped crackers each.*

**Substitute:** Don't have canned crabmeat? Use 1 (6 oz.) can white tuna in water instead.

**Nutrition Information Per Serving:** 90 calories, 6g total fat, 2.5g saturated fat, 140mg sodium, 7g carbohydrate, 3g protein.

# ROAST BEEF, ARUGULA AND BLUE CHEESE TOPPERS

Prep: 10 min. ● Total: 10 min.

12 **TRISCUIT** Rosemary & Olive Oil Crackers

12 baby arugula leaves

 3 thin slices deli roast beef (about 2½ oz.), quartered

 1 Tbsp. **KRAFT** Light **ROKA** Blue Cheese Reduced Fat Dressing

 3 grape or cherry tomatoes, quartered

**TOP** crackers with remaining ingredients.

**SERVE** immediately.

*Makes 1 doz. or 4 servings, 3 topped crackers each.*

**Substitute:** Prepare as directed, using thinly sliced leftover cooked roast beef or steak.

**Nutrition Information Per Serving:** 110 calories, 4g total fat, 1g saturated fat, 120mg sodium, 11g carbohydrate, 7g protein.

# MANDARIN ALMOND-CHICKEN BITES

Prep: 10 min. ● Total: 1 hour 10 min. (incl. refrigerating)

½ **cup finely chopped cooked chicken**

½ **cup drained canned mandarin orange segments, chopped**

¼ **cup dried cranberries**

2 **Tbsp. PLANTERS Sliced Almonds**

2 **Tbsp. MIRACLE WHIP Light Dressing**

48 **TRISCUIT Crackers**

**MIX** chicken, oranges, cranberries, almonds and dressing; cover.

**REFRIGERATE** at least 1 hour.

**TOP** each cracker with 1 tsp. of the chicken mixture just before serving.

*Makes 4 doz. or 16 servings, 3 topped crackers each.*

**Make Ahead:** Chicken mixture can be stored in refrigerator up to 24 hours before spooning onto crackers as directed.

**Nutrition Information Per Serving:** 90 calories, 3.5g total fat, 0.5g saturated fat, 110mg sodium, 12g carbohydrate, 3g protein.

## Jazz It Up:

**Garnish topped crackers with a parsley sprig.**

# RITZ HOLIDAY BELL

Prep: 10 min. ● Total: 10 min.

- **6** slices **OSCAR MAYER** Hard Salami
- **1** pkg. (6 oz.) **KRAFT** Cracker Cuts Mild Cheddar Cheese
- **18** **RITZ** Crackers
- **18** thin red pepper strips
- **2** tsp. chopped fresh parsley

**CUT** 3 small bell-shaped pieces out of each salami slice and 1 small bell-shaped piece out of each cheese slice, using small cookie cutter or sharp knife.

**TOP** crackers with salami and cheese.

**DECORATE** with the peppers and parsley.

*Makes 1½ doz. or 6 servings, 3 topped crackers each.*

**Fun Idea:** Not sure what to do with the cheese after the cutouts are removed from the cheese slices? Fill them with additional salami bells and place on top of additional **RITZ** Crackers.

**Nutrition Information Per Serving:** 120 calories, 9g total fat, 4g saturated fat, 260mg sodium, 6g carbohydrate, 5g protein.

## Jazz It Up:

Use a variety of small, holiday-shaped cookie cutters such as trees, ornaments and stars for a festive look.

# TASTEFUL
# TRADITIONS

**Classic desserts made better by adding
your favorite cookies "all dressed up"**

# EASY CHOCOLATE ÉCLAIR SQUARES

Prep: 30 min. ● Total: 3 hours 30 min. (incl. refrigerating)

- **2** cups cold milk, divided
- **1** pkg. (4-serving size) **JELL-O** Vanilla Flavor Instant Pudding & Pie Filling
- **1** tub (8 oz.) **COOL WHIP** Whipped Topping, thawed
- **22** **HONEY MAID** Honey Grahams
- **4** squares **BAKER'S** Unsweetened Baking Chocolate
- **¼** cup (½ stick) butter or margarine
- **1½** cups powdered sugar

**POUR** 1¾ cups of the milk into large bowl. Add dry pudding mix. Beat with wire whisk 2 min. Gently stir in whipped topping. Layer one-third of the grahams and half of the whipped topping mixture in 13×9-inch pan, breaking grahams as necessary to fit; repeat layers. Top with remaining grahams.

**MICROWAVE** chocolate and butter in medium microwaveable bowl on HIGH 1½ min., stirring after 1 min. Stir until chocolate is completely melted. Add sugar and remaining ¼ cup milk; stir until well blended. Immediately spread over grahams.

**REFRIGERATE** at least 4 hours or overnight. Store any leftover dessert in refrigerator.

*Makes 24 servings, 1 square each.*

**Nutrition Information Per Serving:** 180 calories, 8g total fat, 5g saturated fat, 170mg sodium, 27g carbohydrate, 2g protein.

## Latte Éclair Squares:

Prepare as directed, substituting ¾ cup chilled, brewed, double-strength MAXWELL HOUSE Coffee for ¾ cup of the milk used to prepare the pudding.

# RITZ ANGEL PIE

Prep: 15 min. ● Total: 45 min.

 3 **egg whites**

½ **tsp. vanilla**

 1 **cup sugar**

24 **RITZ Crackers, finely crushed (about 1 cup)**

 1 **cup finely chopped PLANTERS Pecans**

¼ **tsp. CALUMET Baking Powder**

1½ **cups thawed COOL WHIP Whipped Topping**

**PREHEAT** oven to 350°F. Beat egg whites in large bowl with electric mixer on high speed until soft peaks form. Blend in vanilla. Gradually add sugar, beating after each addition until well blended. Continue to beat until stiff peaks form. Mix cracker crumbs, pecans and baking powder. Add to egg white mixture; stir gently until well blended. Spread into greased 9-inch pie plate.

**BAKE** 30 min. Cool completely.

**TOP** with the whipped topping just before serving. Store any leftover dessert in refrigerator.

*Makes 8 servings, 1 slice each.*

**Nutrition Information Per Serving (with raspberry sauce):** 310 calories, 16g total fat, 4g saturated fat, 125mg sodium, 41g carbohydrate, 4g protein.

## *Jazz It Up:*

Toss 1½ cups (about half of 12 oz. pkg.) frozen raspberries with 2 tsp. sugar in microwaveable bowl. Microwave on HIGH 30 sec.; stir until raspberries are thawed and sugar is dissolved. Place in blender; cover. Blend until smooth. Strain to remove seeds, if desired. Drizzle over pie just before serving. Garnish with a few fresh raspberries.

# WHITE & BLACK-TIE-AFFAIR PIE

Prep: 30 min. ● Total: 5 hours (incl. refrigerating)

**57** **NILLA** Wafers, divided

**2** Tbsp. sugar

**¼** cup (½ stick) butter or margarine, melted

**2** cups cold milk, divided

**1** pkg. (4-serving size) **JELL-O** White Chocolate Flavor Instant Pudding & Pie Filling

**1** tub (8 oz.) **COOL WHIP** Whipped Topping, thawed

**1** pkg. (4-serving size) **JELL-O** Chocolate Flavor Instant Pudding & Pie Filling

**2** squares **BAKER'S** Semi-Sweet Baking Chocolate

**CRUSH** 35 of the wafers. Mix crumbs with sugar and butter until well blended. Press firmly onto bottom and up side of 9-inch pie plate. Pour 1 cup of the milk into medium bowl. Add dry white chocolate flavor pudding mix. Beat with wire whisk 2 min. or until well blended. (Mixture will be thick.) Add 1 cup of the whipped topping; stir gently until well blended. Spread evenly onto bottom of crust. Top with 12 of the remaining wafers.

**POUR** remaining 1 cup milk into separate medium bowl. Add remaining dry pudding mix. Beat with wire whisk 2 min. Gently stir in 1 cup of the remaining whipped topping; spread evenly over wafer layer. Refrigerate at least 3 hours. Meanwhile, melt chocolate as directed on package. Dip one-third of each of the remaining 10 wafers in chocolate. Turn wafers slightly, then dip the opposite side of each wafer in chocolate, leaving a V-shaped portion of each wafer uncoated in the center. Use a wooden toothpick to decorate wafers with some of the remaining chocolate to resemble bow ties. Add "buttons" with small drops of the remaining chocolate. Place on wax paper-covered baking sheets; let stand until chocolate is firm.

**TOP** pie with remaining whipped topping just before serving. Garnish with decorated wafers. Store any leftover dessert in refrigerator.

*Makes 10 servings, 1 slice each.*

**Nutrition Information Per Serving:** 340 calories, 16g total fat, 10g saturated fat, 450mg sodium, 48g carbohydrate, 3g protein.

## Jazz It Up:

Garnish with colored sprinkles just before serving.

# HOLIDAY "EGGNOG" SQUARES

Prep: 15 min. ● Total: 3 hours 15 min. (incl. refrigerating)

**67 NILLA Wafers, divided**

**¼ cup (½ stick) butter or margarine, divided**

**2 Tbsp. sugar**

**3 squares BAKER'S Premium White Baking Chocolate**

**2 cups cold milk**

**2 pkg. (4-serving size each) JELL-O Vanilla Flavor Instant Pudding & Pie Filling**

**¾ tsp. rum extract**

**¼ tsp. ground nutmeg**

**1½ cups thawed COOL WHIP Whipped Topping**

**CRUSH** 35 of the wafers; place in medium bowl. Melt 3 Tbsp. of the butter. Add to wafer crumbs along with the sugar; mix well. Spoon into 9-inch square pan; press firmly onto bottom of pan. Set aside.

**PLACE** chocolate and remaining 1 Tbsp. butter in small microwaveable bowl. Microwave on HIGH 1 min. or until butter is melted. Stir until chocolate is completely melted and mixture is well blended. Drizzle over crust.

**POUR** milk into large bowl. Add dry pudding mixes, extract and nutmeg. Beat with wire whisk 2 min. Gently stir in whipped topping. Spread half of the pudding mixture over crust; top with 16 of the remaining wafers. Cover with remaining pudding mixture. Refrigerate at least 3 hours or until firm. Cut into squares just before serving. Garnish with the remaining 16 wafers. Store any leftover dessert in refrigerator.

*Makes 16 servings, 1 square each.*

**Nutrition Information Per Serving (without cookie dipped in chocolate):** 210 calories, 9g total fat, 5g saturated fat, 280mg sodium, 31g carbohydrate, 2g protein.

# *Jazz It Up:*

Prepare dessert and refrigerate as directed. Meanwhile, partially dip the remaining 16 wafers in additional melted BAKER'S Premium White Baking Chocolate. Immediately sprinkle coated portions of wafers with sprinkles. Let stand until chocolate is firm. Store at room temperature until ready to use as directed.

# NILLA TORTONI "CAKE"

Prep: 20 min. ● Total: 4 hours 20 min. (incl. freezing)

1 pkg. (12 oz.) **NILLA** Wafers, coarsely crushed, divided

1 cup **PLANTERS** Slivered Almonds, toasted, divided

1 container (1¾ qt.) vanilla ice cream, softened, divided

½ cup caramel topping

**SPRINKLE** 1 cup of the wafer crumbs and ⅓ cup of the almonds onto bottom of 9-inch springform pan; top with half of the ice cream. Repeat layers of the wafer crumbs, almonds and ice cream. Top with remaining wafer crumbs and almonds; press into ice cream with back of spoon to secure. Cover.

**FREEZE** at least 4 hours.

**REMOVE** side of pan before cutting dessert into wedges to serve. Drizzle with caramel topping. Store any leftover dessert in freezer.

*Makes 16 servings, 1 wedge each.*

**Substitute:** Prepare as directed, substituting your favorite flavor ice cream.

**Nutrition Information Per Serving:** 280 calories, 14g total fat, 5g saturated fat, 150mg sodium, 37g carbohydrate, 5g protein.

## How to Toast Nuts:

Spread almonds into single layer in shallow baking pan. Bake at 350°F for 5 to 7 min. or until lightly toasted, stirring occasionally.

# OREO CHOCOLATE CHEESECAKE

Prep: 30 min. • Total: 6 hours 15 min. (incl. refrigerating)

38 **OREO** Chocolate Sandwich Cookies, divided

5 Tbsp. butter or margarine, melted

5 squares **BAKER'S** Semi-Sweet Baking Chocolate, divided

1 pkg. (8 oz.) **PHILADELPHIA** Cream Cheese, softened

½ cup sugar

1½ cups **BREAKSTONE'S** or **KNUDSEN** Sour Cream, divided

2 eggs

1 tsp. vanilla

2 Tbsp. sugar

**PREHEAT** oven to 325°F, if using a silver 9-inch springform pan (or to 300°F if using a dark nonstick 9-inch springform pan). Finely crush 24 of the cookies; mix with butter. Press firmly onto bottom of pan. Stand remaining 14 cookies around inside edge of pan, firmly pressing bottom edge of each cookie into crust. Set aside.

**MELT** 4 of the chocolate squares in small saucepan on low heat; set aside. Beat cream cheese and ½ cup sugar in large bowl with electric mixer on medium speed until well blended. Add ½ cup of the sour cream, the eggs and vanilla; beat until well blended. Add melted chocolate; mix well. Pour over crust.

**BAKE** 35 to 40 min. or until top of cheesecake is slightly puffed and center is almost set. Mix remaining 1 cup sour cream and the 2 Tbsp. sugar; spread over cheesecake. Bake an additional 5 min. Run knife or metal spatula around rim of pan to loosen cake; cool before removing rim.

**MELT** remaining chocolate square; drizzle over cheesecake. Refrigerate at least 4 hours. Garnish with fresh raspberries, chocolate curls and fresh mint just before serving, if desired. Store any leftover dessert in refrigerator.

*Makes 14 servings, one slice each.*

**Nutrition Information Per Serving (without garnish):** 380 calories, 25g total fat, 12g saturated fat, 300mg sodium, 37g carbohydrate, 5g protein.

# How to Make Chocolate Curls:

Let additional square(s) of BAKER'S Semi-Sweet Baking Chocolate come to room temperature. Carefully draw a vegetable peeler at an angle across the chocolate square to make curls.

# HOLIDAY BLACK FOREST PIE

Prep: 15 min. ● Total: 3 hours 15 min. (incl. refrigerating)

**34** **OREO** Chocolate Sandwich Cookies, divided

**¼** cup (½ stick) butter or margarine, melted

**2** cups cold milk

**2** pkg. (4-serving size each) or 1 pkg. (8-serving size) **JELL-O** Chocolate Flavor Instant Pudding & Pie Filling

**1** tub (8 oz.) **COOL WHIP** Whipped Topping, thawed, divided

**1** cup cherry pie filling

**1** square **BAKER'S** Semi-Sweet Baking Chocolate, melted

**CUT** 10 of the cookies into quarters; set aside for later use. Finely crush remaining 24 cookies; mix with the butter. Press firmly onto bottom and up side of 9-inch pie plate. Refrigerate while preparing filling.

**POUR** milk into large bowl. Add dry pudding mixes. Beat with wire whisk 2 min. or until well blended. (Mixture will be thick.) Spoon 1½ cups of the pudding into crust. Top with the reserved cookie pieces. Gently stir 1½ cups of the whipped topping into remaining pudding; spoon over pie.

**REFRIGERATE** 3 hours. Cover with remaining whipped topping just before serving. Top with the cherry pie filling. Drizzle with melted chocolate. Store any leftover dessert in refrigerator.

*Makes 10 servings, 1 slice each.*

**Shortcut:** Substitute 1 pkg. (6 oz.) **OREO** Pie Crust for the homemade crumb crust.

**Nutrition Information Per Serving:** 420 calories, 18g total fat, 11g saturated fat, 600mg sodium, 64g carbohydrate, 4g protein.

# How to Make Mess-Free Cookie Crumbs:

Crushing cookies into crumbs can be a messy task. To keep the crumbs contained, place the whole cookies in a resealable plastic bag. Squeeze the air from the bag, and seal the bag. Run a rolling pin back and forth over the cookies until finely crushed.

# LEMON-GINGER REFRIGERATOR ROLL

Prep: 20 min. ● Total: 8 hours 20 min. (incl. refrigerating)

**1** cup cold fat free milk

**1** pkg. (4-serving size) **JELL-O** Lemon Flavor Instant Pudding & Pie Filling

**1½** cups thawed **COOL WHIP LITE** Whipped Topping

**30** **NABISCO** Ginger Snaps

**POUR** milk into medium bowl. Add dry pudding mix. Beat with wire whisk 2 min. or until well blended. Gently stir in whipped topping.

**SPREAD** about 1½ tsp. of the pudding mixture onto each cookie. Begin stacking cookies together, standing on edge on serving platter to make a log. Frost with remaining pudding mixture.

**REFRIGERATE** at least 8 hours or overnight. Cut diagonally into 12 slices to serve. Store any leftover dessert in refrigerator.

*Makes 12 servings, 1 slice each.*

**Make Ahead:** Be sure to refrigerate this dessert at least 8 hours before serving to allow the cookies to soften to the desired cake-like texture.

**Nutrition Information Per Serving:** 130 calories, 3g total fat, 1.5g saturated fat, 260mg sodium, 25g carbohydrate, 2g protein.

# HONEY MAID GINGERBREAD HOLIDAY HOUSE

Prep: 1 hour ● Total: 1 hour

- ½ cup powdered sugar
- 1¼ tsp. water
- 9 squares **HONEY MAID** Gingerbread Grahams
- 18 squares **POST** Honey Nut Shredded Wheat Cereal
- 4 pieces **POST GRAPE-NUTS O'S**
- 2 Tbsp. **POST** Fruity **PEBBLES** Cereal

**MIX** sugar and water. Add small amount of additional water, if necessary, to make a very thick frosting; spoon into small resealable plastic bag. Cut small piece from one of the bottom corners of bag to use for piping frosting; set aside.

**ASSEMBLE** house, using 1 of the grahams for the floor and 4 of the remaining grahams for the walls, securing with frosting. Cut 1 of the remaining grahams diagonally in half; attach cut-sides of graham halves to opposite sides of house to form roof supports. Attach 2 of the remaining grahams with frosting to form roof, sealing all edges with frosting. Let stand until set.

**CUT** remaining graham to use for door and 2 windows; secure to house with frosting. Attach shredded wheat cereal to roof for shingles and **GRAPE-NUTS** to top of roof for chimney, using frosting to secure. Decorate with **PEBBLES** Cereal to resemble lights, wreath and walkway, attaching with frosting as needed.

*Makes 1 house.*

*The FLINTSTONES and all related characters and elements are trademarks of ©Hanna-Barbera.*

## Take-Along:

This decorative house makes a great gift to bring to a holiday party. Assemble house on a disposable decorative tray or platter; sprinkle BAKER'S ANGEL FLAKE Coconut on tray around house for snow. Stand a few TEDDY GRAHAMS Graham Snacks around house. Then wrap with a large sheet of clear or colored cellophane tied at the top with a festive ribbon.

# GIFT-GIVING FAVORITES

## Great-tasting, innovative gifts from your kitchen

# EASY OREO TRUFFLES

Prep: 30 min. ● Total: 1 hour 30 min. (incl. refrigerating)

1 pkg. (1 lb. 2 oz.) **OREO** Chocolate Sandwich Cookies, finely crushed, divided

1 pkg. (8 oz.) **PHILADELPHIA** Cream Cheese, softened

2 pkg. (8 squares each) **BAKER'S** Semi-Sweet Baking Chocolate, melted

**MIX** 3 cups of the cookie crumbs and the cream cheese until well blended. Shape into 42 (1-inch) balls.

**DIP** balls in melted chocolate; place on wax paper-covered baking sheet. (Any leftover melted chocolate can be stored in tightly covered container at room temperature and saved for another use.) Sprinkle with remaining cookie crumbs.

**REFRIGERATE** 1 hour or until firm. Store any leftover truffles in tightly covered container in refrigerator.

*Makes 3½ doz. or 42 servings, 1 truffle each.*

**Nutrition Information Per Serving:** 100 calories, 6g total fat, 3g saturated fat, 85mg sodium, 12g carbohydrate, 1g protein.

(*Jazz It Up:*
Sprinkle truffles with colored sugar or sprinkles in addition to or in place of the cookie crumbs.

# OREO CANDY CANE BARK

Prep: 10 min ● Total: 4 hours 10 min (incl. refrigerating)

3  pkg. (6 oz. each) **BAKER'S** Premium White Baking Chocolate

15  **OREO** Chocolate Sandwich Cookies, coarsely chopped (about 2 cups)

3  candy canes, crushed (about ¼ cup)

**COVER** large baking sheet with foil; set aside. Microwave chocolate in large microwaveable bowl on HIGH 2 min. or until almost melted, stirring every 30 sec. Stir until chocolate is completely melted. Stir in chopped cookies.

**SPREAD** immediately onto prepared baking sheet. Sprinkle with crushed candy canes; press candy lightly into chocolate with back of spoon.

**REFRIGERATE** 4 hours or until firm. Break into pieces. Store in tightly covered container in refrigerator.

*Makes 1 ½ lb. or 18 servings.*

**Substitute:** Prepare as directed, substituting 10 starlight mint candies for the candy canes.

**Make Ahead:** Bark can be stored in refrigerator up to 2 weeks.

**Nutrition Information Per Serving:** 210 calories, 11 g total fat, 6g saturated fat, 70mg sodium, 27g carbohydrate, 2g protein.

## How to Easily Crush Candy Canes:

Crushing candy canes can be a messy task. To keep the crushed candy contained, place candy canes in a resealable plastic bag and squeeze air from bag; seal. Use a rolling pin or meat mallet to crush the candy into small pieces.

# GRAHAM BREAK-AWAYS

Prep: 10 min. ● Total: 25 min.

**12  HONEY MAID** Honey Grahams, broken in half **(24 squares)**

**½  cup (1 stick) butter or margarine**

**¾  cup firmly packed brown sugar**

**1  cup BAKER'S Semi-Sweet Chocolate Chunks**

**½  cup finely chopped PLANTERS Pecans**

**PREHEAT** oven to 350°F. Arrange graham squares in single layer in 15 × 10 × 1-inch baking pan.

**PLACE** butter and sugar in medium saucepan. Bring to boil on medium heat; cook 2 min. Pour over grahams; immediately spread to completely cover all grahams.

**BAKE** 6 to 8 min. or until sugar mixture is lightly browned and bubbly. Sprinkle with chocolate chunks. Bake an additional 1 to 2 min. or until chocolate is melted. Remove from oven; immediately spread chocolate over grahams. Sprinkle with pecans; press lightly into chocolate with back of spoon. Cool completely. Break into 24 squares; break squares in half to form rectangles.

*Makes 24 servings, 2 pieces each.*

**Substitute:** Substitute **PLANTERS** Cocktail Peanuts for the pecans.

**Nutrition Information Per Serving:** 140 calories, 8g total fat, 4g saturated fat, 90mg sodium, 17g carbohydrate, 1g protein.

## Gift Giving:

Save cookie tins of all shapes and sizes throughout the year. Or buy inexpensive jars, baking pans, mugs or festive serving dishes for packaging your edible gifts. The packaging then becomes a gift too!

# HONEY MAID "GINGERBREAD"

Prep: 10 min. ● Total: 1 hour 10 min. (incl. cooling)

18 **HONEY MAID** Gingerbread Grahams, finely crushed (about 2¼ cups)

¼ cup flour

¼ cup granulated sugar

2 tsp. **CALUMET** Baking Powder

¼ tsp. baking soda

1 cup fat free milk

1 egg, lightly beaten

2 Tbsp. honey

2 to 3 tsp. water, divided

½ cup powdered sugar

**PREHEAT** oven to 350°F. Mix graham crumbs, flour, granulated sugar, baking powder and baking soda in medium bowl. Add milk, egg and honey; stir just until blended. Spoon into 3 lightly greased 5½×3¼×2-inch disposable mini loaf pans.

**BAKE** 30 min. or until wooden toothpick inserted into centers comes out clean. Cool completely.

**ADD** 2 tsp. of the water to powdered sugar; stir until well blended. Add remaining 1 tsp. water if necessary until glaze is of desired consistency. Drizzle over cooled loaves. Let stand until glaze is firm.

*Makes 12 servings or 3 loaves, 4 servings each.*

**Nutrition Information Per Serving (with glaze):** 170 calories, 2.5g total fat, 0.5g saturated fat, 280mg sodium, 34g carbohydrate, 3g protein.

## *Jazz It Up:*

This "gingerbread" makes a great gift to bring to a holiday party. Cool completely and wrap in plastic wrap before placing in a holiday-themed basket or container.

# OREO HOLIDAY TREATS

Prep: 30 min. ● Total: 30 min.

---

8 **OREO** **Pure Milk Chocolate Covered Sandwich Cookies or OREO White Fudge Covered Chocolate Sandwich Cookies**

**Suggested decorations: decorating icings, holiday sprinkles, colored sugars**

**DRAW** stars, trees, holiday ornaments or wreaths on tops of cookies with icing. Decorate with sprinkles or colored sugar, if desired.

*Makes 8 servings, 1 cookie each.*

*Gift-Giving:*

These decorative cookies make a great gift. Remove outer wrapping and plastic tray from original cookie box; line box with parchment paper. Place decorated cookies in mini holiday paper cupcake liners before placing in box. Wrap with colorful plastic wrap and festive ribbon, attaching a candy cane or small holiday ornament to top of package with the ribbon.